10 Key Traits of Top

BUSINESS
-LEADERS-

John Murphy

CONGRATULATIONS AND THANK YOU FOR INVESTING IN THIS BOOK!

While packed with valuable information, I've purposefully written this book so that you can comfortably read it over your lunchtime – probably won't take more than 30 minutes!

Candidly, the information in this short book has the potential to be both life changing and business changing.

These 10 Key Traits of Top Business Leaders can set you on your journey to lasting success.

At the end of this book, you'll notice a section I call– <u>What To Do Next.</u> This details what I recommend as your next steps in transforming your business.

ENJOY AND GROW!

Contents

INTRODUCTION

Forests have been sacrificed to produce the paper for all the books published on leadership – so why have I written this one, and, more importantly, why should you read it?

Well, firstly, I speak from first-hand experience – I have held CEO and Executive Chairman roles in multi nationals for many years. Also, I have been leading my own business, John Murphy International, for the last 11 years and created a global business.

Secondly, I have had the privilege of working closely, as a business coach, to many international businesses, such as, Pfizer, Airbus, Vodafone, State Street Bank, Johnson & Johnson, Carne Group and many others.

For both reasons, I have been fortunate to view leadership from many different perspectives, across a variety of industries, at different stages of their development.

My work, to help support and build leaders and their teams, has enabled me to discover those traits that leaders need to excel in our fast moving world.

I am certain that, embracing these traits, will build your leadership skills and help you – and your team – to perform to the pinnacle of your potential.

So, let's get going!

John Murphy

GETTING AND STAYING AT THE TOP OF YOUR GAME

The good news is you are at the top of your game. Your hard work, persistence, and single minded focus has been recognized and rewarded. Your past performance has earned you a senior leadership position and on paper everything looks great.

The even better news is you could be significantly more productive, even wildly more productive...but you can't do it by yourself.

Leaders face the unique challenge of being evaluated by the Board (or a bank in the case of entrepreneurs) based on the performance of others.

How effectively your team contributes to the goals and vision of the organization is a direct reflection on how well you lead them.

Is your team living up to 100% of its potential? Unless you are the exception, the answer is "probably not."

According to an Interact/Harris poll on Communication Issues that Prevent Effective Leadership employees are not that thrilled with the leadership skills of top management.

Leading complaints included:

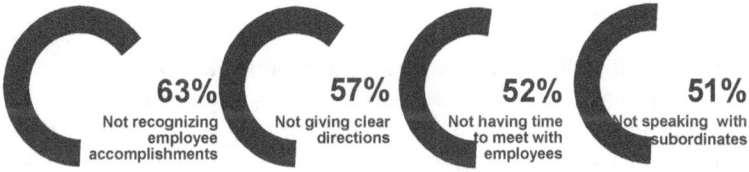

63% Not recognizing employee accomplishments

57% Not giving clear directions

52% Not having time to meet with employees

51% Not speaking with subordinates

• Not recognizing employee accomplishments (63% of respondents)

- Not giving clear directions (57% of respondents)
- Not having time to meet with employees (52% of respondents)
- Not speaking with subordinates (51% of respondents)

Do you see a trend? Imagine how much more productive an organization could become if the percentage of concerned employees could be reduced by as little as 10%? More than that and you would be rocking your industry's world!

Accomplishing that objective is not rocket science. It's a right brain exercise that fully embraces the idea that you lead people and manage things.

It's accepting the idea that leading requires personal communications with everybody on the team; not just the top tier and not just by memos, directives and newsletters.

You as the leader have to be the Chief Evangelist Officer spreading the organization's vision and inspiring all others to buy in.

As diverse as your team is in skills, experience, backgrounds, and culture, imagine the productivity and innovation they can bring to the table if they are all focused, if they are all excited about being focused, on a common goal! You can do it. You wouldn't be where you are today if you didn't have the character and discipline to do it.

You can build a team of happy warriors who sincerely believe that what they do is recognized as having value and that value is multiplied when they support and collaborate with other members of the team.

From comptroller to order picker, everyone will have a common value system as it applies to the organization encouraging increased performance and engendering respect and comradery among the team.

Getting it done does not happen overnight and nobody is going to work harder than you to make it a reality.

However, if you can apply an honest self-evaluation on how you stack up with the following ten leadership traits and make the changes where you need to make the changes, you will be well on your way to a new era of success and personal satisfaction.

These traits are not just for the large multi-national organizations. I have had the privilege of working globally with organizations such as Vodafone, Pfizer, Airbus, Johnson & Johnson, to name a few, who clearly embrace these traits.

I have also worked with smaller, entrepreneurial businesses who, when they develop these traits, they leave their competitors in their wake.

So no matter what size you are now, these traits are the cornerstone of your success!

#1. VISION

Let's start by agreeing that "vision" is a snapshot of what the organization wants the business to look like in the future.

The vision is the raison d'etre for the organization's existence and to make the vision a reality everyone has to buy into it.

Most especially you as the leader have to buy into it.

The vision has to completely resonate with you because your job will be to spread that vision with a passion among members of your team.

It's time for a gut check.

- If you own the company then the vision is easy to get excited about it because it is your own.

- If however, you are a C Suite leader and the "vision" is not crystal clear to you, if it doesn't provide the inspiration and targeted direction you need, then there is no way you are going to effectively inspire your team.

If you find yourself in that position, and many do given the number of "vision statements" that are generated by corporate communications departments, then you need to resolve it.

Either find a way to accept it enthusiastically, quit, or create one of your own and hope for the best.

The reasons why you need to do this are compelling:

- The "vision" is the lynch pin of business leadership.

- If you are not a genuine believer in the vision your behavior will reflect that and your effectiveness as a leader will be severely hampered.

But let's assume you are good to go. You believe you work for an organization that mirrors your own values and has the potential to be the finest in your industry. Use that belief to imbue everyone on your team with the same enthusiasm and commitment.

MORE THAN JUST A MOTTO – AN UNDERSTANDING OF PERSONAL VALUE

Too often "vision statements," "mission statements," and organizational tag lines are meant to impress shareholders and customers rather than the people who actually make things happen.

They may be incomplete or overly detailed and they are often times forgotten once the launch party is over, the signs taken down and the lapel buttons stuffed in a desk drawer.

Leaders need to keep the vision alive after the hoopla has settled. The gal on the dock and the guy in data entry has to understand, and believe, that what they do contributes directly to achieving the vision.

As a leader you want all the members of the team to develop a sense of self value and understand how what they do directly impacts the rest of the team in achieving the vision; that goal, that common target that drives all their efforts in one direction.

Developing that sense of purpose is your job. You have to evangelize. You don't have the space for a meeting tent and an organ so your "revivals" have to occur with small groups or one on one interaction.

Remember that people buy into the leader first – then the vision!

Every time you engage a team member is an opportunity to reinforce the "why we are working here" and the importance of their role to the team.

We have spent more time talking about the vision than we will about the other skill traits simply because it is perhaps the most important. Even the best leader is ineffective if he doesn't know where he's leading the people to!

MINI CASE STUDY

An example where getting clarity on vision was so powerful was when I worked with a client, whose business was in the technology world. A key issue was disharmony amongst the top team. After much discussion, we discovered that at the foundation of this issue was a lack of clarity about the company's vision. Once we had everyone pointed in the same direction, the disharmony got diffused.

#2. SERVICE

"Leaders serve and support"
— John Murphy

Have you ever worked for an organization that had an Executive Dining Room? How about an Executive Restroom? I have and I wasn't very keen on the idea. I was told if I worked very hard I could one day access those executive spaces and eat and pee with the elite.

Not my idea of a vision worth pursuing.

When used as an adjective the term subordinate means "lower in rank or position" and that would be a fair description of an organizational chart.

However, when used as a noun subordinate means one who is under the authority or control of another such as an aide, underling, or minion. Used as a verb subordinate means to treat or regard as of lesser importance than something else.

History is full of leaders (both private and public sector) who became classic failures because they believed that subordinates were in fact minions and their only purpose was to serve the brilliant directives of the leader.

In the private sector some of those leaders got fired, some went to jail and in the public sector some were assassinated.

LEADING IS GIVING

If your team views you as an honest, fair person who treats others with respect, that might qualify you as an ideal next door neighbor but only a reasonable "boss."

Ultimately you want them to see you as a resource whose experience, education, business acumen, personal emotional investment and authority can get them the resources and cooperation they need to better achieve the vision.

To get to that point requires a sincere need to provide service on your part.

Robert K. Greenleaf first coined the term "servant leadership" in 1970. His description of the difference between a "servant leader" and a "leader first" style is illuminating:

"The difference manifests itself in the care taken by the servant-first to make sure that other people's highest priority needs are being served. The best test, and difficult to administer, is: Do those served grow as persons? Do they, while being served, become healthier, wiser, freer, more autonomous, more likely themselves to become servants?"

The benefit of working as a team rather than simply assigning tasks to various components is the synergy experienced resulting in higher productivity.

You are the leader of the team but never forget that you are also part of the team...a very important part of the team.

When you are extolling cooperation and collaboration remember to include yourself in that mix. You may create the guidance but the rest of the team does the heavy lifting. Give of yourself. That means making yourself accessible and sharing your skills with others.

You have a vested interest in your team's success. As a leader, you must serve and support.

By serving the needs of the team and providing the kind of support that you are best qualified to provide, you are serving your own success and building a powerful leadership legacy as well.

MINI CASE STUDY

A CEO in the retail industry hired me to help him engage with his team. When I observed his way of dealing with his people, I suggested that his approach was all about analyzing the results of his team, and nothing about how he supported, helped and coach his people. That one switch, which took a little bit of coaching, transformed his relationship with his people – and their performance!

#3. CULTURE

"Leaders are the evangelists of culture, they carry the torch"

- John Murphy

If the "vision" is what the company is striving for in the future then the organization's culture is an expression of how it's going to behave to get there.

The company culture will manifest itself in particular behaviors, traditions, communication styles, even dress codes.

Some companies may believe that conservative business attire promotes the professionalism, discipline and focus it needs to support its culture while a competing startup company may allow T-shirts and flip flops thinking the casual dress encourages the kind of creativity and innovation it's after.

Which one is right? The marketplace determines that. It may be they are both right for the market niches they are competing in.

One thing that is for certain, the leadership in both organizations has to be the living embodiment of the culture or that successful culture will be replaced, for ill or good, by an organic culture created by the employees.

MORE EVANGELIZING

For your team, you are the company culture. Your decisions, behavior, actions; everything about you will be compared to their perception of what the culture is supposed to be. This is where you need to Walk the Talk and build your credibility.

Leaders are the evangelists of the culture, they carry the torch!

It's also another opportunity to talk up the vision and share your passion for it. It's an opportunity to engage team members one on one and inspire them, fire them up, give them a real sense of purpose.

Corporate culture is one of those nebulous qualities that cannot be completely defined no matter how hard human resources tries to quantify it. You know it when you see it and you notice when it's missing.

Take a look around your team's workspace:

- Does the talk around the proverbial "water cooler" reflect the talk coming out of the board room?
- When people "talk shop" over a cup of coffee does it sound like the same company you work for?

If it doesn't then there is a communications problem or a lack of trust - either way it's a problem that needs to be addressed.

As a leader one of your principal responsibilities is promoting and nurturing the culture and the most effective way to do that is by example. Walk the Walk and invite your team to join you on the stroll.

MINI CASE STUDY

A client in the telecommunications industry asked me to help change the culture of the staff in their branch network. She was horrified when I suggested that that what was happening in the branches was likely a mirror image of what has happening around her top table! Not only horrified, but somewhat insulted, nevertheless she hired me to fix it.

My challenge to her was to start and review the culture of her team – to her credit she agreed. No surprises – the culture in her team was exactly what she disliked in the branches. We focused on fixing her team first – and, hey presto, the culture in the branches then followed!

#4. EXPANSION THROUGH OTHERS

«Leaders ensure their teams shine ,,

- John Murphy

At the beginning of this book we said you would be the person who works the hardest developing a world class team and that's true. But you can't do it all.

As you see progress in the performance of your team you'll realize that its capacity for work has increased.

Nature abhors a void so odds are you will seek out opportunities that allow your team to contribute even more. The good news is your team (in theory) will be even more productive than it was. The bad news is leading the effort will demand even more of your time.

Or maybe not.

EXPANDING YOUR LEADERSHIP CIRCLE:

* How satisfied would you be if you knew you could go no farther?
* How would you react if you knew you were locked into your position with no opportunity to take on new challenges or expand your influence?

You wouldn't be happy. You need to have your own personal vision.

Many of your team members feel the same way. They are all good people and if you want to hang on to them you are going to have to find ways to expand their horizons.

You have to give them opportunities to "taste" those horizons and for some that means taking on leadership tasks that you are doing.

So how do you provide those "tastes" of new responsibility?

You start by making it clear that you support team members who make decisions within their area of responsibility and you shine a light on success stories.

You make it clear to managers and supervisors that delegation can be an effective tool capable of increasing productivity and introducing new ideas to old challenges.

If your company offers leadership training, find a way in the budget to offer it to everyone not just to managers and supervisors.

Uncover that diamond In the rough that was just looking for permission to do more.

Even team members who are natural followers will appreciate that the opportunity was offered even though they have no interest in pursuing it.

Expanding horizons, planting the seed for a team member's personal vision is an essential part of leading the team.

MINI CASE STUDY

When hired by a financial services company to build the team performance, I quickly recognized from interviewing the team that the CEO, who had hired me, was slow to delegate. This caused a bottleneck, but probably more seriously, the team felt they were not trusted by the CEO.

The issue for the CEO was twofold – not having great skills of delegation, but also fear of things not being done his way. Once those two issues were resolved, the team really shone and way outperformed previous results.

Effective leaders make sure their teams shine

#5. STRATEGIC DEVELOPMENT

"The Leaders perspective is from 50,000 feet, not from the forest!"

- John Murphy

According to countless studies and the opinions of senior shareholders this is the big one.

Strategic thinkers, people who can project out how an action will affect internal departments as well as customers and vendors, and determine the sustainability of the action, are perceived as being far more effective and having greater potential value to an organization than those who score low on strategic thinking.

Strategic thinking differs from strategic planning in that strategic thinking is an everyday mindset:

- It's a long range approach to problem solving and decision making that requires analyzing how a decision will impact the entire "business puzzle" 6 months from now, a year from now or even 5 years in the future.
- Strategic thinkers may also be tactical thinking, results oriented leaders but tactical thinkers are not necessarily strategic thinkers.

ARE YOU LOOKING AT THE BUSINESS FROM 50,000 FEET OR 500?

There's a reason why strategic thinkers are something of a rare breed despite the fact that they are perceived as having high value.

Today's business culture places a premium on "right now" as opposed to sometime in the future. Making this quarter's numbers or this month's or even this week's has become the mantra in many organizations.

Results oriented, tactical thinkers are best suited for achieving those immediate objectives and often times their compensation is based on that performance.

But there has to be a strategic thinker evaluating the decisions of the tactical thinker to ensure those actions will have a positive long term effect on the vision.

The true leaders' perspective is from 50,000 feet, not from the forest! Is that you?

STRATEGIC THINKERS ARE VORACIOUS CONSUMERS OF INFORMATION:

- They make a point of staying current on the activity of the competition, identifying the biggest and the up and coming customers in the market, technology advances in the industry, even the performance of vendors.
- They pay the same attention to the various departments within their own organization to identify trends and relationships created by recent actions.

Is this your cup of tea or do you take a more parochial approach?

You don't need to be a strategic thinker to be a great team leader, but you need to understand the concept particularly if your own decisions meet challenges from others in the organization.

However, if you consider yourself a strategic thinker, or you are striving to become one, can you list specific daily habits or routines that support that position?

MINI CASE STUDY

A friend of mine, who is the CEO of a very entrepreneurial start up software development business, came to me to ask for help. Her issue was simple – but it caused her worry! – she recognized that she was good at the idea creation and then taking the next steps to implementation but had really no longer term strategy.

What she lacked was not the skill – she is one bright lady, I can tell you! – but a process. Once we created the process together, and mapped out how this would be reviewed on an ongoing basis, she was, and is, off and running.

#6. IMPLEMENTATION

"Leaders get things done – with speed!"

- John Murphy

Brilliant ideas, your own or those that have been passed down to you from above, only become truly brilliant once they have been implemented.

It's your job as the team leader to ensure the idea becomes a reality without diminishing the "shine" on the brilliance.

Strategic projects often involve enterprise solutions that can require a significant change in the way business is done.

Obviously it is important that you as the leader fully comprehend the project and understand how it contributes to achieving the vision. When you have that clear in your mind, it's time to convey that understanding to the team and spell out your plan for implementation.

THINK BACK TO YOUR LAST MAJOR IMPLEMENTATION PROJECT

• Did your last project go smoothly?

• Did you learn anything about implementation from it?

• How did the end results stack up to your expectations?

When implementations go south it is usually because one or more of the critical leadership responsibilities failed somewhere along the line.

It's incredibly important that you communicate not only the procedural steps but the "why" the implementation is occurring in the first place.

CLARITY IS THE KEY.

You want your team to fully comprehend how the project compliments and promotes the organization's vision and how it assists them in accomplishing their goals.

Before you turn them loose, make sure they understand what you have said. Ask them what the project will mean to them and the team.

Ultimately it is your responsibility to get this project out to the marketplace quickly.

Confusion in the implementation of a project can cost time and that can have serious implications for other departments, customers and vendors.

Your job is to guide the process and provide whatever your team requires to accomplish the task successfully.

Implementation will probably require resources not available in the day to day operation of your team.

It is the leader's responsibility to provide the support needed to accomplish the task and to run interference if there are conflicts with other departments.

DELEGATING responsibility for milestones is critical and those leadership selections may not be obvious.

For example if the implementation is an enterprise software your Manager of Distribution may be brilliant but teaming him or her with an engineer from IT as a "translator" may not only smooth out the task but improve the performance of the software as a result of the collaboration by two people from different disciplines.

And then there is the team leader.

Part cheerleader, part monitor, full time source of inspiration, the leader works like a general contractor tracking progress, troubleshooting and ensuring the project comes in on time and on budget.

Nobody said this job was easy.

Remember, true leaders get things done – with speed!

MINI CASE STUDY

A team I was working with in the pharma industry complained that everything in their company seemed to take too long to get completed. There was a culture of blame bouncing around – but no one was taking responsibility.

Not surprisingly, when we did some analysis, we discovered the fault clearly lay within the team itself. Two clear issues jumped out.

Firstly, the output form the projects they complained about were not crystal clear – there was slight, but important, differences of opinion, as to what a successful outcome looked like.
Secondly, there was a poor level of holding each other accountable. There was an unspoken, never admitted, underlying agreement that if I don't challenge you, then you won't challenge me.

Once removed, things got done better – and faster!

#7. PASSION

"A Leader without passion is no leader at all"

~ *John Murphy*

Everyone has a passion for something, but in today's recovery, jobs are not high on the passion meter.

Even before the difficulties of 2008 many people saw their employment as a means to earn a living that allowed them to do things they had a passion for. Today, for too many people, a job is simply a means to survive.
But, you have a passion for your job or you wouldn't be in the position you are in today.

We're not talking about fanaticism but rather a sincere belief in both the organization's vision and that the work you do is important to achieving that vision.

You don't need a cheerleader because you are already committed to what you do. But have you shared that passion with your team?

A leader without passion is no leader at all!

NO AWE INSPIRING SPEECHES REQUIRED – JUST A TRANSPARENT CONVICTION IN YOUR BELIEFS

It would be nice if you were a talented motivational speaker and you could come up with a "Remember the Titans" talk on demand.

But, perhaps you're not, and neither are most other passionate leaders. Most passionate leaders don't consciously display their passion, they simply live their commitment.

From a team member's perspective, what are their expectations of a leader?

- A leader that is obviously honest in his commitment to the vision,
- Is not dogmatic and welcomes discussion about the organization's direction,
- Walks the talk,
- Leads by example, and
- Stays committed to his beliefs during difficult times
- Is a leader who is passionate about what he or she is doing.

Remember when we said you have to promote the organization's vision and culture with the vigor of an evangelist?

Being perceived as having a sincere passion for what you are saying is the juice that gives you credibility among your team.

When leaders are truly passionate, people will feel like they are truly included in the leader's commitment and are making important things happen for the organization.

That feeling, that sharing of the leader's passion is very powerful and long lasting. Tap into it!

MINI CASE STUDY

The CEO of a major brewery tasked me to work with the Sales Director and his team. The team was underperforming, and the reasons were not clear. After working with the team for a short period, I was coming to the conclusion rapidly that the issue lay with the Sales Director.

He was skilled, articulate and bright. But, between an assessment of his Emotional Intelligence and a series of interviews I ran, it was clear that he was not passionate about his role. To him, it was just a job!
He was neither passionate about the job, nor the company – nor even indeed the industry! Clearly, the role and he were not suited to each other.

We worked with him over a period to help him find another industry and role more suited to him – thankfully, it worked out for all concerned.

The message was clear – you cannot fake passion, and when it is missing it really impacts upon performance!

#8. RESPONSIBILITY

"Leaders accept responsibility – they do not blame"

– John Murphy

This one goes in two directions; both require self-confidence and a measure of courage.

In the old Army, the advice to enlisted people was "never volunteer for nothin'."

In today's business environment the opposite is true.

Seek out opportunities to take on new responsibilities if you are confident you can handle them.

Don't husband your team's talent and resources. If you are not at full capacity seek out projects that can benefit from the services your team can provide that further the vision.

This can result in a couple of things:

- Firstly, you can be viewed by senior leadership as the committed go- to person when an important project needs somebody to shepherd it through completion.

- Secondly, your team will assume some of that reputation and feel like the team that was always a contender now playing for the World Cup Final or the World Series.

There is a down side of course. If you have overreached, if the additional responsibility results in less than stellar performance, you, not your team is responsible.

But that's not all bad if you own up to it.

NEVER HAVING TO SAY YOUR SORRY – GREAT MOVIE LINE, LOUSY IDEA IN BUSINESS

Responsibility is a two edged sword.

When things go right it's nice to get the credit but when things go wrong the conventional wisdom among too many leaders, especially aspiring leaders, is to find a spin that deflects responsibility or accepts responsibility conditionally.

You know these people, we all do.

Many politicians have turned avoiding responsibility into an art form often referred to as "Teflon" where everything negative just slides right off them.

What they seem to be unaware of is their behavior is obvious and does nothing to improve their reputation.
In business there are three very powerful words that not only enhance your personal reputation but also demonstrate to your team and others that you put honesty and honor above personal protection and those three words are "I was wrong."

It takes courage to admit you are wrong and it takes a sense of humility to apologize to those that were affected by your mistake. Mostly it takes a personal moral code that places a high value on integrity.

If you think about those traits, honesty, honor, courage, and integrity you have just identified four highly desirable leadership characteristics.

From a team member's perspective, a leader that doesn't hesitate to take responsibility for mistakes is one that can be trusted. In fact a leader who doesn't put self-protection above the interests of the organization can inspire a culture of solidarity, openness to change, and innovation.

We are not suggesting that you look for opportunities to fail so you can make strategic apologies but we are suggesting that taking responsibility can be an important part in developing an effective and cohesive team.

Leaders accept responsibility – they do not blame!

MINI CASE STUDY

A couple of years ago I got a call from the Managing Partner of a professional services company who wanted to meet. This meeting turned out to be one of the most refreshingly honest meetings.

His opening line went something like this: "I started this business from my back bedroom and now I have 8 partners and we employ over 60 people. However, I recognize that I am the wrong person to be running this business now, but don't know where to go next – can you help?"

Helping him was the easy bit – that was simply putting a process in place to find the right person and get the team working together efficiently.

The hard bit he had done on his own – he had taken responsibility for the underlying issue, and took action! A great example of taking personal responsibility.

#9. COACHING

"Leaders coach their people to arrive at destinations they have never experience before"

— *John Murphy*

Do you remember the mentor that helped you along early in your career?

- How important was he or she to your professional development?

- Was there a supervisor who took you aside and gave you tips and timely feedback on the work you were doing?

- Did those coaching sessions help you expand your horizon?

Of course you remember them and of course the time and attention they gave you helped shaped your later success.

The big question is, how much time are you putting in "paying it forward?" Coaching is an integral part of leading. Coaching is an important key to optimizing productivity organically.

When members of your team feel respected and have a sense of self value that you imbue through coaching, they become motivated, confident, innovative and committed.

They are more likely to be willing to confront challenges, adapt to change and most importantly, view their work as purposeful and a valid contribution to reaching the vision.

COACHING TAKES TIME YOU CAN'T AFFORD NOT TO SPEND

In Olympic team sports there is only one person who goes by the title Coach. There are several assistants but the players will refer to them by attaching last names to the title like Coach Elliot, Coach Smith, and Coach Williams to distinguish between them. But when a player says "Coach told me..." that can only mean the ultimate leader had spoken.

In your team you are "Coach." So:

- How much attention you pay to individuals and what you say carries weight among the team members?
- Are you using that prestige wisely?

You have the talent and the position to be an agent of change for your team. You have the talent and the position to be an agent of change for your team.

You can instill self-confidence in your team members and inspire them to take the initiative in problem solving, thinking creatively and assuming ownership for their areas of responsibility.

The benefits of effective coaching will show up as increased productivity but more importantly, you will have a highly motivated unit ready to take on challenges with the knowledge that together they can do nothing but excel.

Leaders coach their people to arrive at destinations they have never experienced before.

Coaching takes time and a sincere engagement with others. Can you honestly say you are investing the time and talent needed to yield the potential benefits?

MINI CASE STUDY

I can give no better example than my own personal experience. When I first became a manager, I imitated the actions of my own manager, and focused on my team's activity, outputs, results etc. Wasn't that my job? The results were pretty ok – hitting target etc, but not out of the park. Someone I respected suggested I hire my own coach – and purely out of respect for that person, I did.

I owe so much to that decision! My coach now taught me one of the greatest lessons I have ever learned – his mantra was, and is, "you coach and lead people, you manage things".

Taking that mantra on board changed my life – and the results that that, and future, teams delivered.

#10. PRESENCE

Have you ever been in a meeting when the speaker turns to you and asks your opinion and you have no clue what he is talking about because your mind was running a hundred miles per hour thinking of other things?

That's what we would call a "lack of presence" and that condition is all too common.

Leaders influence others by their presence, which endures in their absence.

Our everyday life is full of mental distractions and we have become acclimated to speeding up the "listening" process by using our prejudices to predict both the importance, and often times the outcome, of "listening" sessions we engage in with others.

For example when Bob asks you about a budget problem inside your brain you are thinking "it's just Bob whining again" or "that can't be done" or "the answer is to outsource" before Bob has finished his question.

At work, poor listening skills can cause errors, delays, missed deadlines, erode relationships and is not conducive to team building.

As the leader you not only have to develop excellent listening skills but encourage them in others.

WHEN YOU ARE LISTENING, BE SURE ALL OF YOU IS ACTUALLY THERE

The biggest expense associated with effective listening is time, yours and the people you are engaged with.

You need to develop a method that allows you to clear your mind of extraneous noise and focus on what is being said. Actually if we all developed that skill the world would run much smoother, but right now we are focusing on you.

Think back to the last conversation you had. If it was face to face did you establish and maintain eye contact or were your eyes focused on something else?

If the conversation was by phone:

- Did you multi-task checking email or schedules while your conversation ran on?

- Did you interrupt the speaker rather than waiting for a pause?

- Did you really hear everything that was said or was your mind already shaping what you think the content of the conversation is?

It's important that you be totally engaged in a conversation; not just for the sake of accuracy but also for developing your personal brand.

If your team members start saying things like "I can't talk to that guy," "he never listens to me," "it's like talking to a brick wall," "there's no use talking with the guy," then they really will stop talking to you and that marks the beginning of the end of your effectiveness as a leader.

Think about that the next time someone says "have you got a minute."

MINI CASE STUDY

Recently, I coached a senior director in an advertising agency, and through that coaching an issue arose that was a real stumbling block for her in her role. The issue transcended both her professional and personal life. It became clear that she needed to share this with her boss. But when I raised it her answer was: "Can't do – if you mention anything that remotely relates to a personal life, he just switches off and you know you have lost his attention".

I had noticed the same thing when talking to her boss – anytime you mentioned something he disliked, or was not important, he dismissed it or even ignored it.

I did challenge him on it and, to his credit, he was not aware of it, but took responsibility and did something about it.

The relationship changed for both of them.

WHAT TO DO NOW?

Thank you for reading this book, The 10 Key Traits of Top Business Leaders, and it is likely that, having absorbed all this valuable information, the question in your mind is – what do I do now?

I'm glad you asked!

Remember, at the very beginning of the book we talked about getting and staying on top of your game? Well, let me ask you a few questions?

Would you like:

• Your team to be more productive?

• The level of individual accountability to be much higher?

• Your team to be better at holding each other accountable?

• All of you to be aligned on the key issues?

• Open and challenging debate to become the norm for your team? Imagine what the impact on your business would be even if a few of these changes became a reality?

If you are interested in higher levels of productivity, accountability and greater alignment, I invite you to take a look at my website **www.johnmurphyinternational.com** where there is a load of content that can help. There you will also find our contact information and how we work with businesses across the world be more effective and become more profitable.

I typically engage with clients with in three different ways:

1. **One on One Private Coaching** – I work remotely and/or face to face with top executives around the world to become more effective leaders

2. **Top Team Programs** – I help teams achieve more, deliver greater results and create a culture of speedy implementation. This is done through onsite, bespoke team programs

3. **Individual Project Work** – Where a client reaches out to deliver specific projects. Examples can be strategy workshops, change programs, vision and mission development, among others

Please feel free to connect with me in the following ways:

• Through my website, **www.johnmurphyinternational.com**

• By email at **john@johnmurphyinternational.com**

• Or link directly to my schedule to find a time at **http://www.meetme.so/JMIOnlineMeeting**

3 MOST COMMON SPEEDBUMPS TO PROGRESS:

I have been very fortunate to have worked with many companies worldwide over a wide range of issues that include: teamwork, strategy, culture, behavior, implementation, goal setting and other such items.

What I have learned from many successful engagements is that some of them almost never happened!!

As a strategist and a business consultant I have asked many questions and listened to many top executives and I have discovered that many of these successful engagements almost did not take place for the following reasons, and some, or all, may resonate with you:

1. He is not an expert in our industry
2. Don't want to wash our "dirty linen" in public!
3. Don't know if such an intervention will work

Well, let's talk about the first one. As an industry leader yourself, you know that expertise in strategy development, team efficiency, culture and implementation transcend all industries, geography, ages and gender. That is where we are strong as we have worked across all those terrains.

Secondly, you don't want to share your problems with outsiders. I understand that, but to allay any fears, when you decide to engage with John Murphy International, we will sign a Non-Disclosure Agreement. This guarantees that any information shared with us remains within the boundaries agreed.

Lastly, you don't know if such an intervention will work. That is a reasonable concern and, until such time you become a client, I cannot answer that fully.

However, to help you in this thought process, I invite you to do 3 things:

1. Visit my website, **www.johnmurphyinternational.com**, where you will see many testimonials from past clients.
2. Google "John Murphy International". In this day of freedom of information and openness, any bad press is available to all. Our reputation is fully intact!
3. I invite you to schedule a free 30 Minute Private Consultation – and this is at no cost, not any obligation, and is purely exploratory. This call is for our mutual benefit. Let me explain. The way I have grown my business over the last 12 years is that I have only taken on clients where a) I believe there is a great opportunity for success, and b) where there is a "fit" between the client and I. This consultation will enable you to see if you are comfortable with my approach, and if we have a strong case for delivery of success.

To organize that consultation, please email my assistant ces@johnmurphyinternational.com who will arrange to get you on my schedule.

Alternatively, you can access my scheduler here - http://www.meetme.so/JMIOnlineMeeting.

P.S If you would like to get an audio version of this book, then go to my site to access it now. Click here – www.johnmurphyinternational.com.

JOHN MURPHY BIO

I'm John Murphy and I had a long, and thankfully, successful career at the top of the corporate ladder where I held various roles which included Sales Director, CEO and Executive Chairman.

Why is that relevant to you? Well, my experience allows me to step into your shoes very easily and see the world from your perspective – I have been there and done that!
I am an experienced business coach who focuses on helping CEOS, business owners and top teams build sustainable businesses. I am passionate about working with my clients to help them identify what is holding them back, and then building an enterprise that flourishes.

I coach top business teams in a wide range of industries, and on an international basis. I help teams understand what is holding them back from delivering what they are capable of, eliminate the blockages to success, create trust and ensure focus on what matters most to the business.

I am also an expert in Emotional Intelligence. I incorporate this into my work to help my clients have a better understanding of their effectiveness and performance in everyday life.

http://johnmurphyinternational.com/

 http://twitter.com/jmicoaching

 http://www.facebook.com/johnmurphy.focuspoint

 https://fr.linkedin.com/in/johnmurphyinternational

 https://itunes.apple.com/ph/podcast/winning-at-business-and-life

10 KEY TRAITS OF TOP

BUSINESS LEADERS:

HOW MANY DO YOU HAVE